# You C___

MW01595760

# Head (Christ)

# Without the

# Body (Church)

## Diligo Corpus Sarcalogos (Love the Body of Christ)

## T. Charles Brantley M. Div

**Outskirts Press, Inc.**
**Denver, Colorado**

To my wife (Jackie), children (Timothy II and Jocelyn R.) and the Restoration Springs Interdenominational Church family that deal with me on a weekly basis.

To my mother (Ruth Brantley) and sister (Michelle Brantley) and the Greater Love COGIC family (Pastor Eric and First Lady Kendra Johnson) of Tallahassee, Florida who continue the dream of the late Pastor C J Brantley.

Thanks to Charlie Anderson and Richard Bernhardt for initial illustration cover.

Thanks to sam@samwall.com for copybook illustration front and back cover.

Thanks to DJ Buck, Nancy Barrow and Marv (HOT 93.7 FM morning crew) for having me on as their relationship expert and interviewing me about my books.

Thanks to Paul Kretschmer for interviewing me countless times about my books on WIHS 104.9 FM Christian Radio - Connecticut. Thanks also to Rev. G.J. Gerard for allowing me to be on the roster of pastors for the "Bread of Life" WIHS 104.9 FM Christian Radio - Connecticut.

Those who desire seminars, workbooks, CDs and DVDS concerning "You Can't Have the Head without the Body", please contact 203-753-7377.

All Bible Scriptures used KJV.

Thanks to Rev (Dr.) Ken Jones, Dr. Ligon Duncan, and Dr. R. C. Sproul for their love and concern for the word of God. I hope one day to be in their physical presence. This book was inspired by the 2006 Ligonier Conference.

# TABLE OF CONTENTS

# 1 - INTRODUCTION

Today, one of the questions I am asked most frequently is, "Do I really need to go to church?" For many, the answer is no, if you look at their lack of tithes, offerings, and gifts in the body of Christ. This question came into play indirectly when Dr. Ken Jones, during the Ligonier Ministries' 2006 National Conference, spoke on the visible church. In his address, he mentioned that the body of Christ is as important as the Christ. They work in tandem. *Habeas Corpus* is the church. *Habeas Corpus* means 'you may have the body' in Latin. Yes, we have the body, and it is the church.

From the 1900s to today, places of worship have increased in size from small houses to coliseums. During this evolution, many have missed the mark of the church and have redefined the church to their own gain. It seems like the spirit of relativism, pragmatism, positivism, humanism, secularism, and pluralism has redefined the definitions of Christian and church. Yet, I stand to say the definition has not changed. If Jesus is the same yesterday, today, and forevermore, so is His church. The church is a place of fellowship and a time to seek the Lord.

I have heard many say, "I do not need the church" because of crooked pastors or members that were in the last body fellowship. Because of such bad experiences, they say, "I do not have to go at all."

In all of the above excuses, it surely seems that the reasons for NOT going were selfish. Yet in Christianity, there is no room for selfishness. There is only room for Christ. If He is Lord, then, whatever He says and does, we must fall in line with His commands. Our morals should line up if we are Christians.

For too long, the world has transformed the church instead of the church transforming the world. I do understand the bending, but you cannot justify the break. In addition, there are great breaks from the gospel in order to court or do a little PR to the public. This is dangerous. As Dr. R. C. Sproul says, our pulpit does not stand on a stage but on a chancel. We must never forget the distinction. Some church people have gone after the world to the point that the church is not even recognized.

First off, the church is what Christ is coming back for. He is not coming back for an individual; He is coming back for the church. In addition, yes, I understand the difference between the invisible and visible church, but Christ is coming for His invisible church. Ephesians 5:27 says, "That he might present it to himself a glorious church, not having spot, or wrinkle, or any such thing; but that it should be holy and without blemish."

The word "church" in Greek is *ekklesia*. The word means "called-out ones." So, yes, Christ is again coming for the "called-out ones." Christ is coming for His body the question is will you be apart of it.

The Lone Ranger was a radio and TV show created by George W. Trendle that premiered in the 1930s. The cast included Tonto, Silver (horse) and the Lone Ranger. Even though called the 'Lone' Ranger he had help. The ranger was not alone. We Christians are no different. We need help and can't fight on our own in this journey called life.

2

If Christ had a posse, we Christians need a posse today. The modern posse is the church. (www.answers.com/topic/the-lone-ranger).

Christ set the example of the church by assembling men to help Him preach the gospel. Please note that Jesus did not need any help. The Bible says He had twelve legions of angels at his disposal (Matthew 26:53). Yet He, Jesus the Christ, wanted men to get in their spirits the power of more than just one person. He assembled men who would in turn flip the world upside down. Jesus, in other words, set the example.

In addition, we all know that His 12 members did not all get along. Some were good while others were crooked and selfish men, but He still let them remain a part of his group. Jesus did not kick them out of the church, nor did the disciples leave Jesus for another prophet. They stayed right there.

Jesus even said in Matthews 18:20: "For where two or three are gathered together in my name, there am I in the midst of them." Jesus said that if two or three get together He would be in the midst. Note its more than one person gathering. Yet in 2008, the Lone Ranger mentality has engulfed many believers. Of course, this is the plan of Satan to keep us scattered and separated.

We cannot let Satan have such glory. We cannot really work as separate individuals. We must learn to pool our gifts and resources together for the glory of Christ. Furthermore, you cannot say you are the only one saved or with revelation. This does not compute. Elijah felt that way in I Kings 19 when Jezebel came after him, but God said there were seven thousands that had not bowed to Baal. In other words, Elijah, get off your high horse because there are others who are saved. This same idiom applies to those who think they are NEO (the one). We are workers together and not alone of the grace and power of our savior.

I say to those who have left the church that you are not the only one. In addition, God commanded you to work with the body. You cannot deny or sweep it away. I need you, and you need me. We are a part of one body in Christ and Christ alone.

As Dr. Jones kept talking at the conference, he said something that had never hit me before. He mentioned the Christ is the head of the body. I have heard this statement repeatedly, but Dr. Jones's statement made a change because if Christ is the head of the church then I cannot deny his body. His statement helped me to focus my attention to the church and not just Christ. The two go together. One can never separate the head from the body. In addition, what has happened is that men have been separating the body from the head for their own selfish or bitter gain. You cannot continue to do such and call yourself a Christian.

You cannot have a body without a head, and you cannot have a head without a body. When people say they do not need the church, they are separating the body from the head. Therefore, in essence, for Christ to function here on this earth, He needs a body. We cannot change the course of nature to fit our needs.

When you deny the church, you deny the head. Thus, you cannot deny His body without denying Christ Himself. You not only deny Christ, but you also deny His work on the cross.

4

Saying "I do not need the church" is saying, "I do not need Christ." Christ is the head of the church. Christ needs the church. Wow, if Christ needs the church, are we better than Christ to tell Him we do not need the church anymore? God forbid.

If Christ needs the church for His function to work, we also need the church. In point, we are the church of God in Christ Jesus. The two parties, Christ and church, must function. This may explain the lack of power in the church because so many are denying the body but accept Christ. You cannot have it both ways: you need both to survive in this world. When we do not acknowledge the church, we only give praise and honor to Satan. We all know that his job is to destroy the church.

Christ has defeated Satan at Calvary. Satan cannot destroy Christ so his next best tactic is to come after the church. Satan does body shots to wound the church. If he can wound the body, he will try to negatively affect the head.

Well, this is the essence of what we have today. People are letting Satan use them to kill the body by division and gossip. Yet the body will survive because the head will survive. No one should want to be a part of the conspiracy to kill Christ again. I do not want to be used by Satan to offend the body of Christ.

I must keep this point going because when you do not attend a local body you are letting Satan win. Actually, you are letting the death of Christ go in vain. This is important because Christ died for the church. He died to leave something behind on this earth. Therefore, because He died He left the benefits to the church. Therefore, when you crucify the church and say you do not need the church, you in turn

5

crucify and say, "I do not need Christ." The church and Christ are inseparable.

In the Old Testament, God DWELT and SPOKE in the tabernacle. In the New Testament, God in Christ DWELLS AND SPEAKS in the church. And, yes, I understand there are personal revelations, but if those revelations mess up the church, there is a problem. You cannot say, "I LOVE Christ and HATE the body." Again, they are the same.

# 2 – HEAD AND BODY GO TOGETHER

When you say, "I love Christ and hate the church," you are guilty of equivocation. When you equivocate, you create ambiguity. In other words, you create two definitions in the midst of the definition. It is like looking at an iron and changing the definition to a broom. You cannot do that.

Well, this explains why church people are messed up. Their mouths say, "I love Christ," but with the same mouth, they say, "I hate the church and want nothing to do with it." This creates problems and pseudo-Christians. This explains why some Christians are so un-balanced: they want Christ but not the church. I am sorry, but the two (Christ and church) are a combo package.

It is a package deal. You cannot hate the one and love the other. When you equivocate, you create uncertainty. Once you create a messed-up definition, you cannot have a life with God. This church is one with Christ. Christ is one with the church.

Scripture demonstrates this in the conversation of Saul to Paul in the New Testament. In Acts 8:1, we read, "And Saul was consenting unto his death. And at that time there was a great persecution against the church which was at Jerusalem; and they were all scattered abroad throughout the regions of Judea and Samaria, except the apostles." In verse 3, we also read, "As for Saul, he made havoc of the church, entering into every house, and haling men and women committed them to prison."

We see in the two verses that Saul went after the church. He persecuted the church to destroy it. This was the statement from Dr. Jones that excited my interest. Saul wanted to hurt the church but also wanted to cause havoc on the church. Please notice that nowhere do you see Christ in these verses.

Saul thought he was attacking only the church. He thought he was killing only the church members. He thought he was cursing only the church. He thought he was talking only about the church. He thought he was gossiping about the church. However, it was not just the church; it was Christ, too, that Saul was hurting. Verse 1 states that the persecution involved the church. However, every swipe, hit, and killing of the saints was not just against the church but also against Christ. Christ and the body (church) are one.

Saul wanted to put the church into prison. He wanted to hurt the church in a big way. His goal was to tear down the church. His goal was to put the church in its place. However, look as we see further in scripture that in actuality Saul was also putting Christ to hurt and pain.

In Acts 9:1, we read, "And Saul, yet breathing out threatening and slaughter against the disciples of the Lord, went unto the high priest," This is where the plot gets interesting because Saul is about to go to Damascus to do more harm. Saul was ready to do harm but along the way, Christ speaks to him. Look at what Jesus says to Saul in verse 4.

In verse 4, we read, "And he fell to the earth, and heard a

voice saying unto him, Saul, Saul, why persecutes thou me?" Verse 5 says, "And he said, who art thou, Lord? And the Lord said I am Jesus whom thou persecute: it is hard for thee to kick against the pricks."

The above verse is also seen in Galatians 1:13 for it says, "For ye have heard of my conversation in time past in the Jews' religion, how that beyond measure I persecuted the church of God, and wasted it [.]"

**Please look and see that Christ did not say, "Saul, you are persecuting the church."**

Christ did not say, "You are hurting the church."

Jesus said, "You are hurting me."

In addition, in the course of the conversation Saul said, "Who are you?" He was clueless that he was hurting the Christ. People are clueless today when they take their gifts and offerings and put them on the shelf which in turn negatively affects the church.

We cannot forget the parable when Jesus talked about the man who buried his God-given gift. Do we remember the judgment upon him in Matthews 25? Jesus not only rebuked the man but put him into eternal damnation.

I do not know what your judgment will be, but if you are not using your God-given talents (gifts), you are hurting the church. There is no way you can be heard or please God in this condition. And when you hurt the church, you hurt Christ.

Oh, how many people have left the church they were attending because it was headless. They had the preacher, singing, choir, and gifts, but Christ was not the head. As important as the body is, so is the head. If Christ is not the head, it will scare all away from the power of God.

Charisma, money, building funds, choir, and exegesis of the Word cannot take the place of Christ being the head. No Christ, no church; no church, no Christ. All work in tandem.

The following additional scriptures talk about how Christ and the church are one.

Romans 12:5 say, "5So we, being many, are one body in Christ, and every one members one of another."

1 Corinthians 12:12 and 27 say, "12For as the body is one, and hath many members, and all the members of that one body, being many, are one body: so also is Christ. 27Now ye are the body of Christ, and members in particular."

Colossians 2:17 says, "17Which are a shadow of things to come; but the body is of Christ."

My brothers and sisters, we cannot get around it. The body is needed as Christ is needed. We cannot kick the body to the curb. We cannot state that it is a broken model. We need to bless the body (Church). When we bless the body, we bless the Head (Christ).

You cannot have the Christ without the body. Dr. Ligon Duncan said people are hostile to corporate worship. He added people could get dissatisfied with 10% of the church and search for the 10% but in the meantime lose the 90%

and this becomes an ongoing entity chasing a pipe dream.

There is no church that is perfect unto itself. Christ twelve disciples were not perfect. If Christ was able to deal with it so should we.

Christ was able to endure and tolerate a messed up bodies of believers. Not only did he endure them but he sufferer with them after his resurrection and their maturing in the gospel. But they **suffered** <u>awhile</u> to **reign** in <u>eternity</u>. How can we be in Christ the head if we suffer nothing? Yes, the biggest suffering may be in the church but this is where you will start the reigning because you ENDURED.

1 Peter 5:10 says "But the God of all grace, who hath called **US** unto his eternal glory by Christ Jesus, after that ye have **SUFFERED A WHILE,** make you **PERFECT, STAB-LISH, STRENGTHEN, SETTLE** you."

We have the answer to why Christians are leaving church and their faith. They leave because they don't know how to suffer a while. They move at the slight point of problems, disagreements and discomfort. <u>**Yet the fruit of such creates an imperfect, un-established, weak and unsettled Christian.**</u> Oh people of God, if we want to be strong you must suffer awhile. If you want to be perfect you must suffer awhile.

Running makes weak and not strong Christians. If Christ suffered among his own, we must suffer the same among our own.

# 3 – SPIRITUAL STROKES

Because of TV, many people ONLY eat "TV dinners" and believe that these are still healthy meals. TV dinners are never good in comparison to the real thing. TV dinners have a lot of salt in them. In many cases, the amount of sodium is double a person's daily need.

In addition, as we all know, too much salt is not good for you. In the flesh world, too much sodium will cause hypertension and high blood pressure.

Well, the same is said in the spiritual world. Too much spiritual salt correlates to unsound teaching from nothing but TV religious programming. In addition, if you continue to eat such meals, you will have a spiritual stroke and possibly deteriorate in the faith.

As a physical stroke encumbers, so are Christians with spiritual strokes who eat (learn) only TV religious programming. A stroke restricts your ability. We have Christians who are limited in their talking and walking with God because they live on a constant diet of TV religious programming.

Therefore, when they eat ONLY TV DINNERS, Christians are not really growing. Their diet affects them so much that they will not take correction, and their gifts waste away, and or they become corrupt or Jezebels.

In addition, I believe it bothers God that one uses their gifts for the secular world, but when it comes to church, they take a chill pill. You are hurting the local body when you do not use your gifts. When you hurt the body, you hurt the head. When you hurt the church, you hurt Christ.

Back again to Acts 9, Jesus said, "You have hurt me, Saul." I hear God saying the same thing today to those who refuse to go to church. When you say, "I do not need the church," you also say you do not need Jesus. The church and Jesus are one. They work in tandem. This conversation between Paul and Christ was so powerful that it was mentioned two more times. He speaks on it in Acts 22:5-8 and Acts 26:10-15.

Acts 22:5-8 says, "As also the high priest doth bear me witness, and all the estate of the elders: from whom also I received letters unto the brethren, and went to Damascus, to bring them which were there bound unto Jerusalem, for to be punished. In addition, it happened, that, as I made my journey, and was come nigh unto Damascus about noon, suddenly there shone from heaven a great light round about me. In addition, I fell to the ground, and heard a voice saying to me, Saul, Saul, why persecute you me? In addition, I answered, who art thou, Lord? And he said unto me, I am Jesus of Nazareth, whom thou persecute."

Acts 26:10-15 says, "Which thing I also did in Jerusalem: and many of the saints did I shut up in prison, having received authority from the chief priests; and when they were put to death, I gave my voice against them. In addition, I punished them oft in every synagogue, and compelled them to blaspheme; and being exceedingly mad against them, I persecuted them even unto strange cities. Whereupon as I went to Damascus with authority and commission from the chief priests, At midday, O king, I saw in the way a light from heaven, above the brightness of the sun, shining round about me and them which journeyed with me. And when we were all fallen to the earth, I heard a voice speaking unto me, and saying in the Hebrew tongue, Saul, Saul, why persecutest thou me? It is hard for thee to kick against the pricks. In addition, I said, who are you, Lord? And he said, I am Jesus whom you persecute."

I believe there is a powerful reason why Paul mentioned this conversation three times. He wanted to show the intensity of his actions of hurting and offending both Christ and his church.

How can you hate the church when God adds to it. If God hated the church he would not add to it. Acts 2:47 says, "Praising God, and having favor with all the people. And the Lord added to the church daily such as should be saved."

Do you see this? The Lord added to the church. It was neither people nor custom; it was God who added. Now if the Lord did not want the church to grow or if He felt there was no need for the church, He would have subtracted. But He did not subtract, He added.

Now if God added, how dare people talk subtraction or dividing as it relates to the church? How will judgment day be when Christ does the tally and says those affected negatively than positively as it relates to the church?

# 4 – CHURCH FULL OF SINNERS

I can hear people saying, "The church hurt me, and it left me bitter because of the people within." As I heard, Dr. Ligon Duncan say, "The Lord himself said that there would be false prophets and wolves in sheep clothing. If this were not true, then Jesus would be a false prophet. The fact that there are false prophets and hurtful people in the church just means that Jesus was a true prophet and prophesied correctly." This is a profound statement from Dr. Duncan. Therefore, if there is no hurt or pain in the church, then in reality it is not a church.

Because Jesus said that there would be pain, this should put our minds at ease. It should make us chill and understand that Jesus said that, in His church, there would be wheat and tares, and He commanded them to grow together. Again, how dare I go against what Jesus said? I should not say because of the pain or falseness I will stop going to church. No, in fact, I will do just the opposite. I will understand the word of God and take the pain, and move on.

As it relates to the wheat and tares, Matthew 13:24-30 says, "24parable put he forth unto them, saying, The kingdom of heaven is likened unto a man which sowed good seed in his field: 25while men slept, his enemy came and sowed tares among the wheat, and went his way. 26when the blade was sprung up, and brought forth fruit, then appeared the tares also. 27the servants of the householder came and said unto him, Sir, didst not thou sow good seed in thy field? from whence then hath it tares? 28said unto them, An enemy hath done this. The servants said unto him, Wilt thou then that we go and gather them up? 29he said, Nay; lest while ye gather up the tares, ye root up also the wheat with them. 30both grow together until the harvest: and in the time of harvest I will say to the reapers, Gather ye together first the tares, and bind them in bundles to burn them: but gather the wheat into my barn."

Dr. Duncan also said that we should not forget that the church is full of sinners. He mentioned that the church is the only institution that wants bad people. The church wants those who are wrong and those who admit they are wrong. By their admission, they are at the foot of the cross. The problem comes when people think they are perfect and they have no need of the cross. When people fall into that category, you know they will start to hurt the church with their gossip and their mouths. Again, when you hurt the church, you hurt Christ.

Let us quickly look at Jesus' crew again. He had all types of people in this 12-member church, but they were problem children and demon seeds. In fact, an insider killed Jesus. Notice that Jesus still kept Judas as a part of the body. **Now if Christ was able to tolerate Judas and if Judas was able to tolerate Christ, what is our problem today in the body of Christ?** How can you tell Christ that you are leaving the body when He tolerated Judas?

There is no perfect church. This bears repeating again. All are sinners SAVED by grace in a church. We are all WORKS in progress. Jeremiah 17:9 says, "The heart is deceitful above all things, and desperately wicked: who can know it?" Since we all have issues, let us bring them to the church. The book of James tells us to confess our sins one to another (James 5:16). Yet if you have no local body, whom do you confess too?

# 5 - TOLERANCE

Whether you understand it or not, grace and mercy are nothing but God TOLERATING YOU. If we could really see that, our whole lives would change. If we could see God tolerating us, we would take such a different look at those around us.

Luke 10:37 says, "And he said, He that shewed mercy on him. Then said Jesus unto him, Go, and do thou likewise." Do you see what the Master said after given the parable of the Good Samaritan? He said go and do likewise. Jesus told the people go and show mercy to another. Any Bible scholar will tell you that the Samaritans were arch-enemies of the Jews. Yet Christ still said to show mercy to them. Well, if God showed mercy, what is our problem? If God loved, what are our issues in life?

If Jesus said, "Show mercy," then we who are in the body of Christ need to show mercy to another person. Our Christianity is not based on our shouting and running. It is TOTALLY based on how we treat one another. It is said that they will know who we are by our love. If there is no love, there is no Christianity. Remember, Jesus said take the mercy that you learned and do likewise. What has happened is that people have taken the way of the Pharisee and Levi. The Pharisee and Levi left their fellow brother on the road. The Pharisee and Levi left him for dead. We must unlearn the way of the Pharisee and Levi.

**How many former church members have you and I left**

**for dead? Even as I write this, I ask for forgiveness from any I have harmed. I pray those who read this booklet will do the same.**

How many have said, in essence, "I know the pastor is wounded, I know the church is wounded, I know the church needs my help and assistance, yet I will not help. I will not assist the body." However, do you see what God did? Though the Pharisee and Levite left their fellow brother for dead, God took a foreigner and stranger, and brought forth salvation.

Oh men and women of the most high God, who have we left for dead? What church did we leave wounded? Yes, I know you were wounded by the church, but can I ask, how did you leave? Did the pastor apologize or was he or she humbled? In addition, after even the pastor apologized, did you leave? After repenting, did you still take your talents and tithes away in disgust? If God gives us mercy what is wrong with us giving it back to others especially those of the household of faith. We MUST to learn to show mercy to others.

The following scriptures point out the power of being an example of the mercy of God toward others:

John 13:15 says, "For I have given you an example, that ye should do as I have done to you."

1 Peter 2:21 says, "For even hereunto were ye called: because Christ also suffered for us, leaving us an example, that ye should follow his steps:"

1 John 3:16 says, "Hereby perceive we the love of God, because he laid down his life for us: and we ought to lay

down our lives for the brethren. Verse 17 says, "But whoso hath this world's good, and seeth his brother have need, and shutteth up his bowels of compassion from him, how dwelleth the love of God in him?" Verse 18 says, "My little children, let us not love in word, neither in tongue; but in deed and in truth."

In looking at 1 John 3:16, how much plainer can you get? John says the saints ought to lay down their lives for one another. However, in 2008, people are leaving churches in droves and not laying down their lives for anyone.

The main reason Christians are not laying down their lives for others is because many are commercial or professional. Professional Christians means when things are going well and the pots are "full" they have no problems following the word of God. Yet when offence or trials come they no longer want to follow the words of our Savior who is the head of the body.

2 Timothy 4:5 says "But watch thou in all things, **endure afflictions**, do the work of an evangelist, **make full proof of thy ministry.**"

How can Christians move from professional to powerful Christians? The answer is in enduring. When you run you are not enduring. And scripture expressively tells us that ONLY through afflictions can we have full proof of the ministry. Many true pastors and members who have stayed in their local bodies can surly attest to making their ministry proven because they went through the test.

The word proof in the greek is *plero' fo' reo'* which means evidence. Where the beef (evidence) Christians? **If the only thing you can show are your "skid marks"** (running fast) versus your "tying another knot" (staying in a local body) you are not making a full proof of your relationship with Christ and his body. My brothers and sisters let us endure so that we can prove not only to ourselves but to the world that we are believers of the way.

# 6 - FORGIVENESS

I know people can be bitter because of the way they were treated at a church. I know another pastor or father may have abused. I know another may have hurt you, but the Lord says to lay down your life for the brethren. If all are saints, then all should act accordingly.

Again, if both you and the pastor repent, why the sudden transfer to another church? I heard Elder Michael Forbes from Faith Center Church of Meriden, Connecticut say when he was in the world and there were fights in the bar, by the next day, the people involved in the fights would buy each other drinks, and all would be forgiven. However, this code of conduct does not exist in the body of Christ for the most part. We fight and part versus fight, heal, forgive and stay.

Yet he said, in the church, let there be a falling out, and people will not speak to another for ages. He said that the bar, in that capacity, had more morals than the church. About this, he is right, and we are wrong.

The bar should not have more forgiveness than the church! **The bar should not be a great place to forgive. After a fight, the same patrons come back again to the same bar, yet in the body of Christ, when there is a falling out parties never speak again to one another or part from the church.** If sinners can still be patrons of a bar after a fight why can't saints of the highest God be patrons of the same church where the fight or disagreement took place. **We all should hold our heads down low in shame for such behavior.**

Again, we should die for another. Too many Christians are leaving AWOL. I do not know if you have noticed, but we are in a war. In addition, when you leave AWOL, you are in trouble with the MSP (military spiritual police). I tell you that the Lord's police are after you.

In addition, sometimes people lie about the Holy Ghost and say, "The Lord is moving me on." No, it is not the Lord all the time, its emotions sometimes. It's "I did not get my way." It's "I am mad at somebody, and I am leaving."

Do I understand that persons have seasons? I say yes. There are always transitions, but hear me. When a pastor or leader speaks a word over you, you should not leave until that word is completed, especially when there is a falling out.

Again, are there bad pastors and churches? The answer is yes, but the majority of churches or pastors are not bad. Together, Christ and the church grow together. God forgives us, and we ought to forgive one another as well.

In point, the church grows because of Christ. God forgive us for the infighting. We must forgive one another.

In 1 John chapter 3 verses 17 and 18, we are told not to shut up the bowels of mercy for one another. Why? Because we are a part of the body. If you hurt or withhold from the body, you also withhold from the Christ. This is not my commandment. This comes straight from God. If we have no mercy, we are not his. This is truth. I must forgive in order forgiven. If I go from church to church because of fights and then demonize the church and pastor after I leave, I demonized also Christ. All are one; we cannot forget that Christ and His body (church) are one.

Can you imagine if after you repented God said no? If after you said, you were sorry God still gave you the judgment of a lifetime. No, God did not do this. He forgave us. So if Christ forgave you, why do you not forgive the body of Christ? Christ has given us an example to follow, so why are we not following it? You must follow the pattern of God.

Jesus did not walk away from you. His word said that WHILE we were yet sinners Christ died (Romans 5:8). If Christ died for you and stayed, why do you leave your church so quickly?

It does not make sense when you have a cut to go further away when the hospital is near.

Too many people when they get wounded leave so quickly they do not even give the church time to apologize and attend to their wound. They just leave, but while leaving, they are "bleeding" to death.

If both the leadership and church ask for forgiveness for not being perfect, why do you turn tail and run away from His body? You need the body, and the body needs you. We need each other, because without the body, we have just a head.

# 7 - SPIRITUAL MURDER

If there is a head, there has to be a body somewhere. In this earthly-zone, we must have a head and a body, and as it relates to the spiritual realm, we must have Christ and the church.

You cannot walk around with only a head. Can you image one walking around with just a head? Walking around with only a head is murder. Well just walking around with Christ (head) but not apart of the body is a crime sir and madam. There is no getting around such. You have committed spiritual murder.

You cannot just walk around with Jesus (head) and not have a church (body). You cannot just walk around loving Jesus (head) and hating his church (body). You cannot hold just Jesus (head). A body (church) must be there. Did not scripture say in Hebrews 10: 5 says "Wherefore when he cometh into the world, he saith, Sacrifice and offering thou wouldest not, but a body hast thou prepared me:"

In conjunction, we have 1 Timothy 3:16, which reads, "And without controversy great is the mystery of godliness: God was manifest in the flesh, justified in the Spirit, seen of angels, preached unto the Gentiles, believed on in the world, received up into glory."

We laugh about the chicken running around with the head cut off but that the church without Christ. Without Christ yes, you have nothing. Without Christ, that church is really a club. However, I submit to you there are more people who love Christ and hate the church than those who love the church and hate Christ. Most people are in the former arena. Yes, they want Christ. Yes, they say give me Jesus but if you want Jesus, you have to have his body as well.

You cannot just walk around with the head and say I am a Christian. NO, you cannot walk in such ignorance or fashion. You must have the body in conjunction with the head.

The head cannot be severed from the body and live. The body cannot be severed from the head and live. If the body is severed from the head, you no longer have a living organism. If the head is severed from the body, you no longer have a living organism. Yes, you need both to live. You cannot have one without the other.

Waking around with Christ without being a part of a local body is murderous. Doing such a deed is a gruesome story. Having just a head and saying that you love Christ dictates you have even decapitated His plan of salvation.

In Dr. Jones message, he brought up the legend of *Sleepy Hollow*. In New England, a folklore story by Washington Irving of a man from Connecticut named Icabod Krane moves to a New York town called Sleepy Hollow. While there, he falls in love with Katrina Van Tassel, but Icabod rival is Grom Bones. Because Icabod is smart, Grom could not by intelligence gain Katrina, but by wit he does because Icabod is caught up in superstition.

On one night Icabod Krane is frightened away by a Headless Horseman to never be seen again. Some believe in the folklore that it was Grom but others believe it was actually a headless horseman.

The point I am trying to say is that seeing a headless horseman was a scary sight so much so that Icabod never came back. Oh, how many people have left Christ because the church they were attending was headless. They had the preacher, choir, and gifts but Christ was not the head. As important is the body, so important is the head.

Charisma, money, building fund, choir, and exegesis of the word cannot take the place of Christ being the head. No Christ no church. No church no Christ. All work in one and tandem.

# 8 – HEAD NEEDS A BODY

If Jesus needed a body for the earth, he still needs a body in the earth, and that body is the church. You cannot take away one from the other. Both are needed in this realm of life. I need the body, and the body needs me. I have to have what God set up. Again, God set up Jesus with a body to do His work. Even though Christ left, His Holy Spirit is given in place. Therefore, if the Spirit of God is here, then the body is here as well.

People could say the church is not needed if Christ did not leave something in place, but He did. He sent the Comforter to lead the body, and so if He left the comforter, the Holy Ghost, He also left the body. This is especially important for those who believe in the spirit (head) but not the body (church).

Oh yea, you can jump, shout, and speak in tongues. Oh yes, you can prophecy and interpret, but if you hate or damage the church, you are going directly against Christ. The spirit of God cannot function without the body. I Corinthians 12 says that. A body is needed to do the work. No body, no work. This is why Paul said in I Corinthians 13 that you can have all these things, but if you have no love, you are nothing.

Hear me, sanctified church. Hear me, gifted people. You cannot love and move in the spirit and hate the church at the same time. You cannot be a part of the power of God in that attitude. You must find a body to operate in. You need both a head and a body. You cannot just have a head.

Ephesians 1:22 says, "And hath put all things under his feet, and gave him to be the head over all things to the church [.]"

Ephesians 1:23 says, "which is His body, the fullness of Him who fills overall."

Ephesians 5:23 says, "For the husband is the head of the wife, even as Christ is the head of the church: and he is the savior of the body."

Colossians 1:18 says, "And he is the head of the body, the church: who is the beginning, the firstborn from the dead; that in all things he might have the preeminence."

You have four scriptures that say repeatedly that Christ is the head of the church. You cannot throw that away. A leader without followers is a man walking by himself. There is a church following Christ. So if you are not a part of the body, then Christ is not your head. You are talking about Christ but not following Christ as it relates to HIS COMMAND to be a part of the local body.

You are operating illegally spiritually when you have only the head but no body (church). Yes, when you re-move yourself from the church, stay home, and do not find a body to work with you, what you are doing is il-legal according to God. Christ is the head of the church.

You cannot take away His body. You cannot be saved and NOT be a part of a church. Do not get mad at me. I am just reading scripture. Christ is the head of the church.

May I humbly add that you SHOULD NOT start a church out of bitterness or strife? The body of Christ has already had enough fractions and splits to last a lifetime. Many have said the growth of churches has been caused by disagreements rather than a divine call or oracle from the Lord (1 Peter 4:11). If one starts a church without divine revelation and counsel, then Christ is not the head; the person who starts that church is really the head.

In fact, if the Lord does not found a church, it is a CULT. Why a cult? Because if Christ is not the head; that man or woman is the head. Make no mistake: Christ must be the head of the church (body).

The word head in the above three verses is *kefale* in the Greek. *Kefale* in Greek means literally the head. According to crosswalk.com, *kefale* also entails that "since the loss of the head destroys life, this word is used in the phrases relating to capital and extreme punishment." In addition, this is exactly what is happening in our churches. People are using the spiritual guillotine.

# 9 – THE GUILLOTINE

The guillotine was a popular form of capital punishment on the neck of its victims during the French Revolution in the late 1700s. During the French Revolution, when the execution was complete, they would raise the head to the crowd, and the crowd would rejoice.

Well, some former members of churches are doing the same thing. These persons leave the church and raise the head of Christ. They walk around with the head to say, "See what I have done. I am walking around with this head, but I have no body at all." This is wrong.

Oh, yes, you have the head, but the body is suffering because it is not CONNECTED to it's head. You must be connected to the local body. You cannot walk around without being connected in some way. A disconnected body is a broken body. A broken body is not a fully functioning body. People of God, we have to be reconnected. We cannot continue to be fragmented.

The guillotine, according to answer.com, was named after Dr. Joseph Ignace Guillotine. He argued that beheading by machine was quicker and less painful than the work of hanging or the firing squad.

This again is happening spiritually all over America. People are leaving the church because they don't "want to hurt the church." They leave because it is a quicker and less painful way. No, my brother and sister, when you leave the body, you hurt the body. There is no getting around it. The head and body are one.

If you have just the head, the body is dead. If you have just the body, the head is dead. Both are needed to survive. I cannot throw out the baby with the bathwater.

Having only the head of Christ is like decapitating Him, which is a horrible thought and sight to ponder. He already died, and now we want to decapitate Him? Now we want to do the cross and the guillotine. No, my brother and sister, we cannot move in this fashion. We must have the body.

Yet any Christian purposely not connected with a church is a part of the guillotine crew.

1 Corinthians 10:31 – 33 says "Whether therefore ye eat, or drink, or whatsoever ye do, do all to the glory of God. 32) Give none offence, neither to the Jews, nor to the Gentiles, nor to the church of God: 33) Even as I please all men in all things, not seeking mine own profit, but the profit of many, that they may be saved."

In verse 32, Paul warns us about offending the "church of God." We cannot continue to offend or cause problems in the house of God and expect God to be joyous. When we offend or hurt the body, we DIRECTLY hurt Christ because he is the head of the church.

Historians say that on some occasions the guillotine's blade had to be used several times on a victim either due to a thick neck or due to the dullness of the blade. For whatever reason, the sight was gruesome. Yet when we continually hurt the body of Christ, we do the same. We are taking the blade up and down until there is a severing of head from body.

Verse 32 uses the word offence. The word offence in the Greek is *ap-ros-kop-os*. The word means "no occasion to sin" or stumbling block. Yet when we put our agenda ahead of God, we may cause another to sin. In addition, when we cause another to sin, we are hurting the body. When we hurt the body or offend it, we hurt Christ as well.

Romans 14:13 says "Let us not therefore judge one another any more: but judge this rather, that no man put a stumbling block or an occasion to fall in his brother's way."

The offence thing is so powerful that Christ even said that if you did it to the least you did it unto me (Matthews 18:5 & 6). Therefore, even in the gospel, Christ was saying when you offended the least you offend Him.

When you take off the head of another brother or sister, or when you wound to the point that the person or church cannot function you have hurt Christ. It is crazy how people say they love Christ but hate their brother. You cannot do both (love and hate).

However, this is the case in some churches. Christians have become bi-polar, without thinking that what they do will hurt another brother and sister. These things are unaccepted in God's kingdom. You must love Christ and his body (brother or sister).

Look at 1 John 3:15 when it says if you hate your brother of sister you are a murderer. This is the word of God. When I take a brother or sister to the guillotine I am a murderer and not apart of God.

2 Corinthians 6:3 says to not give an offense to anyone in the faith. When I cause an offence, I hurt the body of Christ. Such things must not happen in the household of faith.

Acts 24:16 says "And herein do I exercise myself, to have always a conscience void to offence toward God, and toward men."

I believe no other scripture speaks directly to the issue of Christian on Christian crime. We have all heard of black on black crime as the biggest offenders to Afro-Americans. Well, I propose that Christian on Christian crime is the biggest offenders among "Christians". If we take the above scripture in truth, we would not offend. We would not hurt the body of Christ.

When you hurt one in the body, you hurt all. When we take one to the guillotine, we take all to the death. A known fact is that during the French Revolution, people told on each other, which created victims for the guillotine. I believe the same is happening today. It is not the world who judges but Christians who are unjustly and without compassion taking people to their spiritual death.

Yet again, when you offend the least of these you offend Christ. We must get this in our minds. Paul said I would not offend God or man. Moreover, it is not a coincidence that the greatest commandment is loving God and man. If loving God is the greatest commandment than hating either God and / or man is the greatest offense or infraction.

We cannot offend the church (His Body) without offending the head (Christ).

40

# 10 - CRYONICS

Christ already had a horrible death on the cross. How dare we do it again. Herodias (Matthews 14:3-6) took John the Baptist's head from him through the dance of her daughter Salome. In addition, today the spirit of Herodias is working by trying to take the head of Christ off the church. We talk about the spirit of Jezebel, but I believe the spirit of Herodias is more prevalent in our churches because churches are being attacked every day.

Christ is being taken away from His church. People are leaving church to never get involved again with another body. You, sir or woman, have decapitated Christ. Yet, in all Christ will stand, for Christ said in Matthew 16:18 "that upon this rock I will build my church and the gates of hell will not prevail against it."

It will not work. Therefore, we might as well get with the program and march on with a local body.

During the French Revolution, the guillotine killed more than 40,000 citizens. How many have we killed in the body? We must all evaluate ourselves.

Colossians 2:19 says "and not holding fast to the head, from whom the entire body, being supplied and held together by the joints and ligaments, grows with a growth which is from God."

How powerful is this scripture. In the previous verse, Paul said that the people were not acknowledging Christ, and in verse 19, he says the head rests on the body. No head (Christ), then no body (church).

Do not get me wrong. Christ is the main point. In Him, we live, move, and have our being (Acts 17:28). Yet after we recognize the head, we must recognize the body. The head directs the body. If the head is not directing the body, then the body is dead. We must see this same thing in our local churches.

We need both to work. We need Christ, the head, to give us directions. If Christ is not directing you in the local church, then you are not a part of the body at all, plain and simple. No body, no head. You cannot be a part of Christ and not have a body. You need both to function.

In addition, you see people trying to do spiritual cryonics; no, this will not work, either. Freezing the head means that the body is not moving. I am here to tell you the church is a full living organisms. The head needs the body to function properly. No, saint of God, you cannot be in Christ and not be a part of the body of Christ. They all must work in one. There is no freezing going on of Christ.

Colossians 2:19 says that we must hold on to Christ who is the head of His body. The head is in charge. I cannot move without the head. I cannot talk without the head. I cannot function without the head. I need the head, but the head needs the body to function. Both must work together in order to be good.

1 Corinthians 12:12-13, "For as the body is one, and hath many members, and all the members of that one body,

being many, are one body: so also is Christ. 13For by one Spirit are we all baptized into one body, whether we be Jews or Gentiles, whether we be bond or free; and have been all made to drink into one Spirit."

Paul tells us directly that we are one under the banner of Christ. No body will work by taking off the head. You cannot take off the body and expect the head to live. All work together for the glory of the Lord.

# 11 – CHRIST LOVES THE CHURCH

The Father draws us to himself and subsequently puts us in the church (body) according to John 6:44.

Yes, we do not know who is a part of the body (invisible), but I do know once you are converted you are led to a local church. If you are not a part of the local body, then the Spirit of God is not leading you.

Yes, some or all have been hurt and wounded in the church, but that is no excuse to stop going to church. That is no excuse for totally giving up on the plan of God. In conjunction with accepting Christ, joining a church is apart of the plan of God.

Can you imagine if the church had not become a collective body how many schools, hospitals, and other things would not have been built if the church had not come together? We cannot deny the work of the church in years past.

As the church helps this earth in desperate times, so the church needs to come alive with the many things facing our nation. This is not the time to leave the body. This is the time to edify and help the body grow in its proper perspective.

1 Corinthians 12:27-28 says, "Now ye are the body of Christ, and members in particular. 28And God hath set

some in the church, first apostles, secondarily prophets, thirdly teachers, after that miracles, then gifts of healings, helps, governments, diversities of tongues."

Paul here tells us straight up that we are the body of Christ. We work because of Christ. We live in Christ. We are His body. So if we are the body that we must function in a local body. The local body is a part of Christ. To not have a local body is not to have a head, and you are yet dead in your sins.

God did not save you to be alone. God did not save you to be an island. He saved you to be a part of the body of Christ. So the function of the body is important. Without the body, you have no function with Christ. Then your sins are still there, and the judgment of God will be on you because you do not have the Son. Again, you cannot have the Son without the body. They go together. They work hand in hand.

Ephesians 5:29, "29For no man ever yet hated his own flesh; but nourisheth and cherisheth it, even as the Lord the church [.]"

Ephesians 5:30, "30 for we are members of his body, of his flesh, and of his bones." Whom bones flesh and members are we, it is of the Lord.

When we beat the church, we also beat Christ.

When we hate the church, we also hate Christ. When we discard the church, we discard Christ as well. In Verse 29, we see that no man hateth his own flesh. Yes, Christ is Lord of the church. He is not the footnote. He is not the byword. He is not insufficient. Therefore, without Christ, there is no church.

So, since the church will prevail and you are outside that, then you will not prevail. You will not last at all. You will be a byword while Christ and His church will last forever and ever.

Do you see Ephesians 5:25? It says, "Husbands, love your wives, even as Christ also loved the church, and gave himself for it;" My God, the scripture says that Christ loved the church?

The Bible says that Christ loves the church. So how can we hate what Christ loves? How can we repudiate something that Christ is in love with? How can we hate the church when Christ loves it? How can we run from church to church after an offence, and yet when we offend Christ, He stays right there. If God is consistent to you, why can't you be consistent with a local body?

Christ loves his church. We cannot get away from it. Yes, if you love Christ, you must love his church. You must join and be a part of the body of Christ.

When you use your tongue to protest against His body, you hurt Christ. When you use your tongue to take down His body that He loves, you hurt the body of Christ. I must say it again. Christ loves His church. What He loves, we must love. If He is concerned about His church, we must be concerned.

# 12 – ACTIVE PARTICIPATION

If you have the head, then you must have the body in your life. You must understand that the head goes with the body. Again, you cannot just walk around with a head. You cannot be sane with only a head in your hand.

Let's take it deeper. You cannot really walk around with a head because without the body there is no walking, talking, or holding. There is no building, popularity, convocations, speaking engagements, parties, recitals, preaching, prophesying, singing, dancing, speaking in unknown tongues, speaking in known tongues, praise team, dancing etc.

Without a body, the head is in one place standing and doing nothing at all. This is why when a Christian says, "I joined the church," and does nothing, he or she is affecting the body negatively.

Yea, they have Christ, but because they never joined the church or become a true part of the body, nothing really happens because they gave not to the church. When I say 'gave,' I include time, talent, and tithes.

They lied on their tithes; they lied in their offerings, and are repeatedly late and had no respect for the local leadership of the church. Yet they confessed loudly that the church did nothing. In fact, the church did something, but because they were not a part of the body, they did not move.

When the pastor said something, they did not move. When

the church had an outreach, they did not move or get involved. That is not the church's fault. It was their fault, because they disconnected from the source.

Have you ever turned on the light, but the light did not come on? You later discovered that the light was not plugged in. This is the plight of some Christians. They have the light, but there is no power source. They have the vehicle but no gas. They have the house but no home. They must be connected to God and God alone. Yet because they disconnected from the church, Christ HAD to disconnect from them.

The Bible says that God does things in order. The natural order of life is if one major vital part of the body dies the whole body dies. The same with a local body and one person who becomes "spiritual diseased" that affects the entire congregation with 'sickness'.

Therefore, when one sits in the chair and does not actively participate with the church, that person will become disconnected and in return have nothing to show. That person will complain about not having and not really realizing the problem was caused by him or her.

Ephesians 4:15 says without a doubt that Christ is the head of the church. What has happened over time, people take the head but they do not want the body. They praise about how good the head is but they do not like the church. They are not even apart of a local body. They complain about the body and curse it but they want the head. Yet one works with the other. The one cannot work without the other in any way or fashion at all.

I have never heard someone say that I will be paid without

working. The two work hand and hand. You must go to work to be paid. If you do not go to work, you will not be paid. Well, the same is said for Christians who stay home and are not a part of a local body, but they expect to be paid in the end. Those who 'strike' at church may be surprised by their 'reward in heaven.'

# 13 - COMMON GROUND

Ephesians 2:19 states we are fellow citizens of the house of God. I am not an English major, but the's' on citizen means more than one. There is no way one can justify being the lone ranger.

According to His word, we are fellow citizens working together in the house of God (church body). Jesus paid the price so that we could enjoy the church. He paid the ransom so that we could be partakers of His death, burial, and resurrection.

We talk all different dialects but when Christ came and we accepted Him, our dialects and customs changed so that we all could become part of Him. We saw Him and not ourselves. Which raises the following point: how can we disgrace the body? How can we say that we have no fellowship with other Christians when GOD says to be in fellowship? We are fellow citizens with the saints of God.

The verse did not say "fellow strangers." It said "citizens." That means we are in the same nation. We have one king, and His name is Jesus. We have one Lord, which is Jesus. Therefore, in no way will God accept our place in heaven if we have no place on earth. Hear me, brothers and sisters. We cannot enjoy future fellowship with God when we cannot have present fellowship with man on earth. I have a saying: if you cannot get together down here, you are not going to get together up there in glory.

2 Thessalonians 2 says, "1Now we beseech you, brethren, by the coming of our Lord Jesus Christ, and by our gathering together unto him." This, of course, works in conjunction with 1 Thessalonians 4, which talks about the return of Christ.

**If Christ is going to gather His bride on that day, what is the hindrance about being gathered now?** Again, if we are having hard times in fellowship now, what are we going to do on that day? We deal with bad people on our jobs and we tolerate it, yet the body of Christ will fall out by one look and one sour note. We must learn to come together now so that when Christ comes again we will be ready for Him on that day.

We must overcome the works of the enemy and come together. We must find that common ground. Yes, there will be disagreement in the body, but love on. Yes, there will be fights in the body, but love on. We cannot give up on the body. We cannot be happy with the present state of mind that Christ is good and the church is no good. No, the church is still good because God created it by the death of His Son.

No Christian who really understands the relationship between Christ and the church can say, "I do not need the church." You do need the church if you love God and want to please Him. God loves the church, and so should we. God in Christ wants us to take care of the church.

Has the church messed up? Yes, the visible part has, but there is a church within the church. This is called the invisible church. These people are from different church bodies that really love God and are called of Him and at the last trumpet will raise in Christ.

The key is not to figure who is a part of the body or not. The key is to join yourself to a body because you love Christ and want to become a part of the body (church), and in the end, God will reveal those who are His and those who are fake.

# 14 – EDIFY THE CHURCH

1 Corinthians 14:12 says, "Even so ye, forasmuch as ye are zealous of spiritual gifts, seek that ye may excel to the edifying of the church."

Romans 14:19 says, "So then we pursue the things which make for peace and the building up of one another."

1 Corinthians 14:4 says, "One who speaks in a tongue edifies himself; but one who prophesies edifies the church."

1 Corinthians 14:5 says, "Now I wish that you all spoke in tongues, but even more that you would prophesy; and greater is one who prophesies than one who speaks in tongues, unless he interprets, so that the church may receive edifying."

Acts 9:31 says, "Then had the churches rest throughout all Judaea and Galilee and Samaria, and were edified; and walking in the fear of the Lord, and in the comfort of the Holy Ghost, were multiplied."

1 Corinthians 14:26 says, "How is it then, brethren? When ye come together, every one of you hath a psalm, hath a doctrine, hath a tongue, hath a revelation, hath an interpretation. Let all things be done unto edifying."

In the above scriptures, Paul is telling us to edify the church. He is not saying to run from the church. He is not saying to rebuke the church only. He is saying to lift the church up. Paul is saying to put the church up where it belongs. Hear me, please. If Christ is exalted, so is the church.

Again, the church is one with Christ. There is no Christ without the church. Christ will always have a church. So if Jesus is exalted, so is the church. In other words, if you destroy the church you are trying to attempt to destroy Christ.

When we destroy or step on the church, we do the church a disservice. We must edify the church. This must be done in love because Christ loves the church. The church is Christ because, again, Christ is the head of the church. Remember, you cannot have one without the other.

I will admit there are times you *odi et amo* the church. There are times people will cause you to hate and love the church, but you still must let love rule. The trials will come sometimes through church people, but you still must love overall. We must always remember that *omnia vincit amour* (love conquers all).

Paul as the apostle understood the test and trials that the church would go through. He understood the wolves that would come in sheep clothing. He understood the discouragement that would come so that is why he said edify the church.

The word of God says to love His church if you are part of God. They work hand in hand, and the church must be lifted up. You cannot destroy the church without putting a hunting scope on Christ.

Paul even said that edifying the church is more important than having spiritual gifts. If we could stop seeking gifts, titles and just edify the church; if we could just stop looking for the next prophecy and just edify the church. If we could just get out of ourselves and see His glory, we would see the church in its glory.

The church is in His glory, and we must together lift it up to God. The church is *Opus Dei*. The church is the work of God, and we cannot fight against it. We edify God for His work and love toward us. If we can edify His actions, why cannot we edify His creation, the church?

That's why Paul says to build one another up. Because when you build instead of break down, you edify the church. Too many have wounded the church for their own selfish gain. *Alterum non-laedere* says to not wound another. The only way to not wound another is to edify the other.

When you say go up instead of going down, you edify the church. If you do just the opposite and destroy the church, you miss the power of God in your lives and forget how God edified you through His Son.

Yes, maybe you have forgotten, but Christ did edify you from sin and shame. God did lift you up out of your sin and flesh mind. Therefore, if God raised you up, what is the problem in rising up the church? Somebody did not give up on you. Somebody prayed for you until you came to God. If God did that for you, why can't you lift up His church?

Oh, people of God. How wrong it is for God to edify you, and then you turn around, and not edify the body (the church). Yes, the church is a part of God, so when you get down and try to destroy the church, you, in other words, tell God, I did not really appreciate your church.

If He edified you, then it's time to edify your local body by joining and participating. By edifying the local body, you edify Christ Himself. You edify the body by joining and supporting the church.

Again, Paul in the scriptures above says let all things be done unto edifying. He did not say unto profit. He did not say unto personal glory. He did not say unto a building project. He did not say unto a bigger ministry. He says to do all unto edifying. By saying "unto," he is saying let your goal be lifting up the body of Christ. Let your major goal be to help the church stay in the right place and time. We must move on from our own personal growth and see the church. For when the church goes up, you will follow suit.

Ephesians 4:12 says, "For the perfecting of the saints, for the work of the ministry, for the edifying of the body of Christ [.]"

Here again, Paul says to edify the body of Christ. What more proof do we want to keep the church up? What more proof do we need to understand that our goal is not to decapitate Christ from the church? Our goal is to lift the church up. Our goal is to tell the world that the church is our love because Jesus loves the church, too.

Ephesians 1:22 says, "And hath put all things under his feet, and gave him to be the head over all things to the church (1:23) Which is his body, the fulness of him that filleth all in all."

Ephesians 1:22 and 23 shows without question that the church is one with Christ. Christ is the head of the church.

God put all things under the feet of Christ, and GOD made Christ head of the church. The true bishop of our souls is Christ. It does not matter what church you are a part of. Christ is in charge of the Church.

Once again, these two verses UN-mistakenly put together the church and the body of Christ. The head and body are an intimate union. Any one who tries to break up the union is going against Christ. As Christ told Paul you are coming up against me so is anyone who tries to destroy the church. This union will survive. The body is not just one but it is made up of many members. The church is a *pedibus usque ad caput*. From feet to head, the members are needed to encourage the body to higher highs.

# 15 – PRICE OF THE CHURCH

Acts 20:28 says, "Take heed therefore unto yourselves, and to all the flock, over the which the Holy Ghost hath made you overseers, to feed the church of God, which he hath purchased with his own blood."

1 Peter 1:18-19 says, "18Forasmuch as ye know that ye were not redeemed with corruptible things, as silver and gold, from your vain conversation received by tradition from your fathers; 19But with the precious blood of Christ, as of a lamb without blemish and without spot[.]"

Revelation 1:5 says, "5And from Jesus Christ, who is the faithful witness, and the first begotten of the dead, and the prince of the kings of the earth. Unto him that loved us, and washed us from our sins in his own blood [.]"

The above three scriptures show something very powerful. The church is the ONLY thing that Christ purchased. This to me means value. I believe this shows the value of the church. Jesus' blood is valuable. However, He shed His blood for the church.

If God used His Son's blood to buy the church, this tells me that not only does He love the church but purchased it to show His love and value for the church. This was not just lip service; it was also in deed.

Dr. Ken Jones brought this out at the 2006 Ligonier Ministries' National Conference. He was totally right. The church was brought with a price. How dare we then turn around and curse what God has purchased with His Son's blood. How dare we say to Christ what He purchased was no good.

I believe all of us have been victims of people whom we loved for whom we purchased an item, and they turned around and said what we purchased was not good. "It was a waste of time, and I did not like what you purchased."

OK, if you hate that feeling, what do you think and how do you think God feels when we trash His purchase? How do you think He feels when we tell him the church is no good and has no value? No, the church has much value. The church is a beautiful thing that Christ purchased by His own work.

Acts 20:28 says to feed the flock of God (church), which Christ purchased with His own blood. Christ brought the church. Christ paid for the church. So the church does not belong to itself it but to Christ.

If Christ saw value in the church why don't those who leave, discard or abuse the church. If Christ purchased the church than the church belongs to him and not to us. But why do some sell the church at wholesale or as a yard sale. The church is not at discount but at prime. God help those who have a disregard for the purchase (the church) of Christ at Calvary.

# 16 - COMMUNION

Communion is an important part of the Christian experience. Though Catholics believe in the Eucharist (Mass and transubstantiation) and Protestants believe in Communion (non-transubstantiation), the practice is performed in some church every Sunday. The important point is that it is a sacrament that Christ told us to do.

It is a commandment from the Lord Himself. There is no substitution for this sacrament. Yet for the sacrament to really take place, there must be a coming together. Hence, you need a gathering of fellow Christians in a place called a church.

The head (Christ) tells His present and future disciples to come together and remember His death on the cross. This was not an edict or counsel. It is a command from the head of the church. The head of the church, Christ, said, "Come together.' Wow, what more proof do you need to believe that God wants His people to come together? If He tells us to come together for communion, then we should also come together to help and encourage one another as well.

The word communion itself means interacting. If you are interacting with yourself ONLY, then there will surely be a problem down the road. I understand the point of talking to yourself every now and then, but if that becomes your major bread and butter, then you are going to run into trouble. I believe Christ had this idea of communion because He wanted us to come together and encourage one another as well as stay in sound doctrine.

By not coming together in the body, you will have different teaching and exegesis that could corrupt and mess up the minds of believers. Therefore, Christ tells us to come together and communicate.

1 Corinthians 10:16 and 17 says, "16Is not the cup of thanksgiving for which we give thanks a participation in the blood of Christ? In addition, is not the bread that we break a participation in the body of Christ? 17Because there is one loaf, we, who are many, are one body, for we all partake of the one loaf."

Please notice verse 16 when He says, "The bread that we break is a participation in the body of Christ?" You cannot get more detailed in this passage. The communion and the bread part represent the fellowship of the body of Christ. Its participation is important to God. Coming together is what Christ was telling His disciples to do.

1 Corinthians 11:23-29 and 33 say, "23 For I received from the Lord what I also passed on to you: The Lord Jesus, on the night he was betrayed, took bread, 24and when he had given thanks, he broke it and said, 'This is my body, which is for you; do this in remembrance of me.' 25 In the same way, after supper he took the cup, saying, 'This cup is the new covenant in my blood; do this, whenever you drink it, in remembrance of me.' 26For whenever you eat this bread and drink this cup, you proclaim the Lord's death until he comes.33 So then, my brothers, when you come together to eat, wait for each other."

To me, the most important part is verse 33, when He says

to come together to eat. The eating is not just physical but spiritual. You come together in fellowship for the express interest of helping one another to stay in the faith.

Christ told us to do this in remembrance of Him. We come to church for communion, and we come together to fellowship to the glory of God. The communion was to commemorate the Lord's Supper. So, we need the body again. We need the body not only for edifying, but we also need the body for the communion of things.

So, again, when we do not fellowship during the communion, we are hurting the church. The body needs communion. He said, "Come together to remember His work." What excuse can you give now? What statements can you make against the commandment of the Lord? The commandment of the Lord said come together. It is a command of the Lord. It is not an option.

If we partake of Christ body in communion, why not partake of his body in joining a local church. Without a doubt, I believe eating his body means getting involved with the body (church). Jesus the Christ gave the bread to his messed up disciples and said 'take eat this is my body that was broken for you.' I believe Christ also says partake of my body which was broken and left for you (1Corinthians 11:24).

If Christ gave his body to an imperfect church, what is our problem in not fellowshipping with imperfect people? We must follow Christ example.

I believe Christ gave us an allegory when he took the bread and broke it. The church without a doubt has broken issues and promises within it. Yet Christ said partake. Christ himself broke the bread. Christ himself I believe wanted us to see and understand that his body was going to be broken but calls us to function in it. My brothers and sisters we must love his body.

# 17 – NOT ATTENDING CHURCH

If you are not going to church, you are BREAKING a commandment of God. He said come together now. He said come together now for His glory and honor. Dr. Ligon Duncan said, "The invisible church is here and is real, but it's substantially located in the visible church."

**In other words, the invisible church comes FROM the visible church.** If you are not a part of a visible church, then there is a good chance you are not a part of the invisible church.

Dr. Duncan said that most "Christians" have made church like going to the movies, and based on who is preaching, they go to church. Dr. Duncan also said that if Christ was wounded and killed in HIS OWN house by friends and foes alike, why do you think you will escape the same fate in the body. The body wounded Christ.

If the body wounded Christ, we as believers should get in line. This is important because if the will of God was to hurt Christ, why do you think you will escape from it. Therefore, when you are hurt in the body, stop tripping over it and grow in grace.

That is why we have James chapter 1, when it says count it all joy when you fall into diverse temptations. Being wounded in the body does not mean Satan; it means you are a Christian who must be tested.

I cannot talk enough about how so many are going church to church after they are wounded. Instead of running ever time, you must mature and seek God and not your flesh as it relates too being wounded. God wants you to stand still. How many times have we taken a beating at work, but we did not walk off the job in the same frequency as leaving the church? We have to change our minds about this. I do understand the need to move from a church but that in extreme cases or non-repentant pastors, leaders or spiritual season change. Nevertheless, these changes are done in prayer and HUMUALITY. Changes do not come in arrogance, pride, and emotions.

This is why we have communion: to get our minds off one another and on Christ. The more I think about Christ, the less I think about my wounds. When I see his wounds, blood, and body, the less I see of myself. When I see His blood that redeemed me, the less I see mine. This is why we have church. This is why we have communion to change our focus from one another to Him alone.

As long as we see each other, we will hurt and attack one another. However, when we see His nailed hands, feet, and wounded side, our bickering and fighting stops, because we behold the *Agnus Dei.* The Lamb of God is all we need to get through our pain. The purpose of communion is to remember the actions of Christ and take our minds away from each other and place it on Jesus the Christ.

1 Timothy 1:18-19 encourages us to war a good warfare. And yes, the biggest warfare for many begin in the house of God. However, when you do not fight a good warfare your faith can get ship wrecked. This is why Paul tells us to hold fast and not move fast.

1 Timothy 6:12 reminds us to fight the good fight. Yet how can you have a good fight when you run. A fight is not running. A fight is facing your opponent and standing toe to toe with them. Yet Christians don't fight in 2008, they run from church to church. And some get to a point that they don't even go to church anymore. Christians remember we are made to fight and not run. Christians lets not be weary in well doing especially to those of the household of faith (Galatians 6:10). Nevertheless, the question must be asked how can we do well if we are not even in the household of faith.

# 18 - NOT FORSAKING

The last major scripture I use is Hebrews 10:25. It says, "25Not forsaking the assembling of ourselves together, as the manner of some is; but exhorting one another: and so much the more, as ye see the day approaching." I used this scripture last because it is the most used scripture for the defense of going to church. However, I wanted to prove other scriptures relate to Hebrews 10:25.

The first thing that jumps out in verse 25 is 'Not.' In the word of God, we are told not to forsake our coming together. I left this scripture last to be the icing on the cake as it relates to the need to support the local body. We are told in the word of God to not forsake our assembly.

We Christians are funny. We like the Bible when it comes to affecting our pocketbook positively or healing our bodies, but when it comes to a commandment, we have a problem. We must follow orders. It is a shame we follow ONLY the orders or commandments that are convenient but when a charge comes that makes us uncomfortable, we do not follow. The charge is still the same. The head commands us to fellowship. I know without a doubt that people can make things difficult, but Jesus did say, take up your cross and follow me (Matthews 16:24).

The author says at that time, it was a habit already of some Christians to not attend the church. If, in the beginning of church history the importance of fellowship was stressed, how much more today?

The author of the book of Hebrews said to assemble. You cannot assemble apart; you must assemble to get the fire GOING.

When you **BBQ**, you have the coals together to keep the fire going, and so the body of Christ. We cannot just have a head; we must come together to keep the fire going. Without the coming together, the coals will get cold. This may be the hardest thing to face, but when you do not support the body, you will run cold.

This goes back to what Christ said in Revelation 3 verse 15, 16: "I do not want you lukewarm but hot."

When you are hot, you will help another stay hot. Yet when you are cold, unless the other person is hot, you will make others cold. We must work together to keep the body warm. When someone is cold, he or she rubs his or her hands over the body to keep the body warm. This again is our plight in the body of Christ. The more we work and pray together, the warmer we keep the body of Christ. We need each other to stay warm.

The word forsakes means to leave. If you leave, it implies you were there already. It's time to work through things and find yourself not forsaking but helping the body of Christ.

Furthermore, the word "assemble" in the Greek means a complete collection of people. In other words, we are not complete if we are not working and fellowshipping together.

Adam was incomplete until he had Eve. Well, the Bible tells us that the Christian is incomplete until he or she is filled not just with God's Spirit but connected with a local body. In addition, not just a part of the body of Christ but working fully and completely.

# 19 – RIDING SHOTGUN

Hebrews 10:25 mentions the word 'ourselves'. This means among OTHER Christians. Walking by yourself is not the key; it's walking and fellowshipping with one another.

Many have heard of the phase "riding shotgun" without understanding its meaning. Shotgun was a reference back to the stagecoach days when the driver of the stagecoach could not watch out for bandits and crime, so another person's sole job was to ride with the driver and look for the enemy with his shotgun. They had to work together to survive.

Yes, I know you need Jesus, but you also need company and reinforcement to help the body of Christ. This is why the author says of us, "we need each other." If anything, the devil wants us divided.

When we are divided, we are easy pickings for the enemy to take us off one by one, but together, we have a better chance of surviving. Yes, I know Christ is all you need, but Christ does use people to protect and love you (the church).

When you are in a community of believers, you have more support and reinforcements. Yet, when you are by yourself and not associated with a local body, then Satan can and will have his way with you. Did we forget that even though Christ went away to pray and fast, He AL-WAYS came back to his disciples? (Matthew 14:22-28).

Even when He came back from the dead, Christ came looking for his believers (John 20:26).

How more powerful is that? Jesus the Christ, the most powerful man ever to live still kept up His communion and relationship with others. If Christ can do that, what is our problem? If Christ fellowshipped, what is our issue in life? If Christ was reconnected to His body, why can't we?

What I love about Christ is that He turned around, loved, and ministered to the same people who were not there for him. They all left Him, yet after he was arisen, he ministered to those same people (John 21). What is our problem? Yes, we were wounded in the house of God just as Christ was, yet He came back to the same people who gave Him the scars.

People of God, did not Christ say we would do greater things? Well, why do we only put this in the form of cars and homes? Greater things are also involved in our love and fellowship with one another.

Oh yea, we can please God for crazy things that are tangible, but for some reason, we cannot turn that toward our brothers and sisters. It's time. If the brother, sister, leader, or pastor comes and asks for forgiveness, why not rejoin the fellowship? Nowhere do I see the disciples asking for forgiveness, but Christ still re-fellowshipped with them. Ok, what is our real problem?

Christ has given us the example. The question is will we follow it. Will we plug into the power that God has given His people to deal with attitudes and difference of options? I believe we have the weapon of love and mercy. The question is will we use it to keep the unity of the body of Christ.

78

# 20 – WE NEED THE BODY

I must say again that Jesus gave compassion to His body. We see that in John 20:19. These men had all deserted Christ when He needed them, but He still came back to them after resurrection. Once again, if Christ can and did come back to them, what is our problem? What is our hang-up?

**The body hurt Christ. The body disappointed Christ. The body left Christ. However, Christ came back to the body.** Christ loves the body even after it hurt Him. If such is so, we must take a page and learn from Christ.

**Yes, the body will hurt, but if Jesus can come back and re-fellowship with the SAME group that hurt Him, what is our problem? Jesus did not START ANOTHER CHURCH. If Jesus did not try to FIND NEW DISCI-PLES why do we?** If we have been planted in a church, why do we run away so quickly when an offence happens?

We need the body. Yes, the easy answer is to find another church, but can I say the same problem may happen again at another church? In fact, it does take two to argue, but it takes two mature Christians to come to an agreement and help the body, and not destroy it. Oh, people of God, if Christ did not do a wholesale change, why do we? If Christ did not go to another city and start afresh, why do we? If Christ did not go to another church, why do we?

More so, when Christ left, he gave us the comforter. He, I

believe, gave us an example of how to leave a church. You do not just get up and leave. You do not just pack your bags and go. You always leave something better behind for the church. If Christ left a blessing (Holy Ghost), why do some church members leave a curse or havoc on their former local body?

How can we call ourselves Christians when in the thick of a fight or misunderstanding we act more like the devil than our head (Christ)? Again, Christ loves the body. He came back for it when He was resurrected, and He is coming back for it when He returns in the rapture. We must love the body. We must change from our views to His views.

Even in John Chapter 20, Christ came back purposely for Thomas who would not believe. He came back for Thomas to set the record straight. So should we. This man had the bravery to tell all that could hear that he was not going to believe until he saw. A regular person would have said I do not care, but Christ came back to His brother. The same brother who said he would not believe Christ came back for him, and we should do the same.

Acts 20:7 says, "7And upon the first day of the week, when the disciples came together to break bread, Paul preached unto them, ready to depart on the morrow; and continued his speech until midnight." Please notice that they came together. The scripture does not say they stay separated, but they were together. They forgot about their agenda and came together to fellowship to help and endure the body of Christ.

If this was needed within the first century, how much more in this century of apostasy? We have more ungodly behavior than ever recorded in history, so this is not the time to spread apart but the time to come together in the power of God.

Though we started with verse 25 of chapter 10 of Hebrews, we must look at the two prior verses that read: "23Let us hold fast the profession of our faith without wavering; (for he is faithful that promised; 24And let us consider one another to provoke unto love and to good works [.]"

In other words, the reason why we come together is to make sure our faith does not waver and to ensure that we provoke to love. This explains why Christians who are not placed in a local body are so mean and hard up. They are that way because love is not being provoked. In fact, hate and bitterness are being provoked, and there are no good works to be found.

Here is a great litmus test. If after leaving, is the local body better, is Christ's work being advanced? Are you helping anybody? When people call you from the former church, do you spill more bitterness, or do you help the body? These are good tests. It's funny. People say that the former church was hindering their growth, but once they leave, no fruit is seen.

All is dying on the vine. This again is why when you are offended in the house of God you must not run so quickly. You can do more harm than good if the Holy Ghost does not move you. If you are hurt and the church is not preaching Christ, than run. Yet if the church is preaching Christ and His love, then be led by Spirit and not your emotions.

**Some emotional charged churches are a feeding ground to persons making emotional charged decisions when**

**oughts and offenses occur**. We Christians must remember we are governed by the Word of God and His Spirit and not our emotions.

Again, we need the body of Christ to help provoke us to good works. We need the body of Christ to help us provoke one another to the love of God. Yet when you are separated and not connected to the body, all things of the world will and can affect your walk with God.

As the Word shows, when you are not a part of the body, you will not grow. By not growing, you will die soon. There is no way of getting around that. You need to be a part of the body to grow. This is how we ensure that we hold on to the right profession of faith. It also ensures that we hold fast to the correct teaching of Jesus the Christ.

The reason for so MANY wacky and weird beliefs and denominations is due to people not being a part of the body to be corrected.

This is why some people do not want to go to church or be a part of the body: because they do not want to be corrected.

No one but God can observe and correct them, but this is not the will of God. The Word of God tells us to come together for the edifying. Yet, while you edify, you will may say things to help prune the vine to the will of God or others may say things to you to help prune you as well. No body grows without a cutting process. In addition, unless there is a breaking, tearing, or weakening of the muscle, the body will not grow (John 15:2).

Going to the gym is nothing but tearing down the muscle so

that it will grow again. If you never tear down the muscle, then the body will never grow. This is why the body of Christ is so weak and fractional. We have too many Christians who have not withstood the test of time. Such Christians are gone with one offence or trial within the body. 2 Timothy 4:7 states a "good fight". A fight stipulates you staying in the 'ring'. Yet too many run away with the first punch. Such persons must endure hardness as a good solider of Jesus Christ (2 Timothy 2:3).

Christians who have not endured are constantly breaking under pressure and leaving churches. When the pastor or *emeritus* saint comes and gives words of wisdom, they run from under the covering.

We talk about AIDS, but there is a far worse epidemic in the body of people not holding up under pressure. When pressure or correction comes, they run from the body. This is not the will of God. We must learn and love one another. No diamond or gold is sold unless it has gone through some type of process. No process, no growth. No growth, no gold or diamond.

This is why we must love the body. The body makes us better. Yes, the body can be hard, but together you grow into what the head (Christ) has instructed. We hold to Him because we know Him. In addition, because we know Him we should want to be around like-minded believers to ensure we do not waiver. We want to ensure that we will not fall on that day. We must be strong in His might, yes, but also in the fellowship of the saints of the highest God.

Other scriptures of gathering include 1 Corinthians 5:4, 1 Peter 4:10 and 11, which say to us that we must "minister the same one to another." This is a commandment of God to minister one to another. How can you minister to one another if you do not attend a local body? How can you minister to the next person? We must follow the word of God to the full value. The full value is to put God and His word first. He tells us to forget about ourselves and to minister to each other for the glory of God. When we minister to one another, we help one another. By helping, one another we take each other to the next level of things.

1 Corinthians 8:12 cannot be denied. It says, "12But when ye sin so against the brethren, and wound their weak conscience, ye sin against Christ."

This scripture is direct on my subject of why we need to love the body. When we do not love the body, we will wound the brethren (body). In addition, when that happens, when you wound the body, it says clearly that not only do you wound Christ but you also sin against Him.

The word "wound" means to smite. Smite is another word for hitting or beating. The church takes enough beating from the world. How much more can the church take from its own citizens? This is the point that must be stressed to the highest. By not attending a local body, you only increase the world's condemnation of the church. Is the church perfect? No, it is not. The visible church is not perfect. Yet when we make it our business to become assassinators of an institution that Christ has established, it only demonstrates our lack of love and understanding of Jesus the Christ.

Let this ring in our ears; "When you wound the body you not only wound Christ but you SIN against Christ." With any negativity toward a brother or sister, we have sinned against Christ. The word sin in 1 Corinthians 8:12 is *hamartano* in Greek. The word means to "miss the mark" or trespass. When you trespass on one's property you are subject to get shot. Well the church is the property of Christ, so when you trespass against His body you are liable to get shot 'spiritually' as well.

Matthews 25:40 addresses Christ's statement that when you have done it for the least you have done it unto me. Why can't we get this? When we attack the church and leave it for dead, how in the world do we expect God to be happy about this? We might as well face it. Christ loves the church, and we should love it, too. Love not from a distance but close up. The church needs Christians, and Christians need Christ and the church (body).

# 21 – BRIDE OF CHRIST

In the final analysis of the Church, we have the following scriptures on how the church is the married bride of Christ.

Matthews 25:1-13 say, **"*1*shall the kingdom of heaven be likened unto ten virgins, which took their lamps, and went forth to meet the bridegroom.** *2*five of them were wise, and five were foolish. *3*that were foolish took their lamps, and took no oil with them: *4*the wise took oil in their vessels with their lamps. *5*the bridegroom tarried, they all slumbered and slept. *6*at midnight there was a cry made, Behold, the bridegroom cometh; go ye out to meet him. *7*all those virgins arose, and trimmed their lamps. *8*the foolish said unto the wise, give us of your oil; for our lamps are gone out. [F48] *9*the wise answered, saying, not so; lest there be not enough for us and you: but go ye rather to them that sell, and buy for yourselves. *10*while they went to buy, the bridegroom came; and they that were ready went in with him to the marriage: and the door was shut. *11*came also the other virgins, saying, Lord, Lord, open to us. *12*he answered and said, Verily I say unto you, I know you not. *13*therefore, for ye know neither the day nor the hour wherein the Son of man cometh."

Matthews 22: 1 - 14 says, "*1*Jesus answered and spake unto them again by parables, and said, **2The kingdom of heaven is like unto a certain king, which made a marriage for his son,** *3*sent forth his servants to call them that were bidden to the wedding: and they would not come. *4*, he sent forth other servants, saying, Tell them which are bidden, Behold, I have prepared my dinner: my oxen and my fatlings are killed, and all things are ready: come unto the marriage. *5*they made light of it, and went their ways, one to his farm, and another to his merchandise: *6*the remnant took his servants, and entreated them spitefully, and slew them. *7*when the king heard thereof, he was wroth: and he sent forth his armies, and destroyed those murderers, and burned up their city. *8*saith he to his servants, the wedding is ready, but they, which were bidden, were not worthy. *9*ye therefore into the highways, and as many as ye shall find, bid to the marriage. *10*those servants went out into the highways, and gathered together all as many as they found, both bad and good: and the wedding was furnished with guests. *11*when the king came in to see the guests, he saw there a man which had not on a wedding garment: *12*he saith unto him, Friend, how camest thou in hither not having a wedding garment? In addition, he was speechless. *13*said the king to the servants, Bind him hand and foot, and take him away, and cast him into outer darkness; there shall be weeping and gnashing of teeth. *14*many are called, but few are chosen."

Revelation 19:7-17 says, "*7Let* us be glad and rejoice, and give honor to him: for the marriage of the Lamb is come and his wife hath made herself ready. *8*to her was granted that she should be arrayed in fine linen, clean and white: F31 for the fine linen is the righteousness of saints. *9*he saith unto me, Write, Blessed are they which are called unto the marriage supper of the Lamb. In addition, he saith unto me, these are the true sayings of God. *10*I fell at his feet to worship him. And he said unto me, See thou do it not: I am thy fellow servant, and of thy brethren that have the testimony of Jesus: worship God: for the testimony of Jesus is the spirit of prophecy. 11And I saw heaven opened, and behold a white horse; and he that sat upon him was called Faithful and True, and in righteousness he doth judge and make war. *12*eyes were as a flame of fire, and on his head were many crowns; and he had a name written, that no man knew, but he himself. *13*he was clothed with vesture dipped in blood: and his name is called The Word of God. *14*the armies which were in heaven followed him upon white horses, clothed in fine linen, white and clean. *15*out of his mouth goeth a sharp sword, that with it he should smite the nations: and he shall rule them with a rod of iron: and he treadeth the winepress of the fierceness and wrath of Almighty God. *16*he hath on his vesture and on his thigh a name written, KING OF KINGS, AND LORD OF LORDS. **17And I saw an angel standing in the sun; and he cried with a loud voice, saying to all the fowls that fly in the midst of heaven, Come and gather yourselves together unto the supper of the great God[.]"**

Revelation 21:2, 9-10 says, "*2*I John saw the holy city, new Jerusalem, coming down from God out of heaven, prepared as a bride adorned for her husband. 9And there came unto me one of the seven angels which had the seven vials full of the seven last plagues, and talked with me, saying, Come hither, **I will shew thee the bride, the Lamb's wife.** *10*And he carried me away in the spirit to a great and high mountain, and shewed **me that great city, the holy Jerusalem, descending out of heaven from God [.]"**

Those who still, after reading this booklet, believe there is no need for the church must come to the fact that you cannot have a marriage without a groom and bride. If only one shows up, there is no wedding. You cannot marry yourself. You may be in love with yourself, but you cannot marry yourself. If you have only the bride, you have no wedding. If there is only a groom, there is no wedding.

Without question, the scriptures above demonstrate without a doubt that Christ is the groom. He is going to get married to the one He loves. When a groom makes up his mind to marry a girl, he does not marry a "friend with benefits" or one whom he just lusts after. He marries one that he is DEARLY in love with. He marries a bride to whom if he had to give his life for that bride he would. He is so proud of that bride he even gives her his last name as well as taking responsibility for all debts before the union.

Well, people of God, Christ died for the church. Christ loves the church. Christ will marry the church on the end time of eschatology. He will take the bride and make it not only a union but also a feast for all to see. The invisible church will be that bride. Yet the invisible church is made up of the visible church. Talk about the church, beat the church, kick the church, but Christ is still going to marry the church. Christ is still going to take the church unto His own and make the church His bride.

The bride of Christ will survive. As much as people try to get rid of the church and say it is no good, God has made a promise to this word. The promise is direct and true; there is going to be a wedding feast. There is going to be a gathering of the people of God, and when they gather, those who denied the head and the body will be on the outside looking in.

They will repent not only for their lack of love for Christ but also for their lack of love for the body. You cannot separate the body from the head. The church and the body go together.

It is plain and simple those who make it to Heaven are the

bride of Christ. If you are not in Heaven city, through the shed blood of Christ after His resurrection, then you will not be His bride and will be cast into outward darkness. All the redeemed of God will live in this blessed city. Those who were the invisible church from the visible church will make it to that city.

According to the Dake Bible, this corresponds with John 14:1-3 that says "*1Let* **not your heart be troubled: ye believe in God, believe also in me.** *2*my Father's house are many mansions: if it were not so, I would have told you. I go to prepare a place for you. *3*if I go and prepare a place for you, I will come again, and receive you unto myself; that where I am, there ye may be also." In addition, you have Hebrews 12:23 that says "*23*the **general assembly and church of the firstborn**, which are written in heaven, and to God the Judge of all, and to the spirits of just men made perfect[.]"

There is a great feast coming. The invitations have gone out. The question is, will you be a part of it? The invitations require RSVPs. The invitation I believe begins at every visible church that lifts up the name of Jesus the Christ. This invisible church is ready for a great wedding, but it starts with the visible church. What a shame that the invitation goes out every Sunday and church days, but MANY MANY Christians do not answer the call to come to their own pre-set wedding. Our time at church is only preparing us for our eternal destination.

Only God will know who is a part of His system. It is not my job to find out who is a part of this system.

Only God will have that answer in the end. However, I must start the process. I must be connected to a local body to prepare myself for a day that the earth is looking forward to. The earth wants to see this day come (Romans 8:22). It wants to see the reentry of Eden back on earth in the form of the New Jerusalem. Christ is going to get married. You can fight all you want, but a marriage is going to take place.

The following are more scriptures that talk about the wedding.

2 Corinthians 11:2 says, "For I am jealous over you with godly jealousy: for I have espoused you to one husband, **that I may present you as a chaste virgin to Christ."**

**Romans 7:4 says, "4**Wherefore, my brethren, ye also are become dead to the law by the body of Christ; **that ye should be married to another,** <u>even to him who is raised from the dead</u>, that we should bring forth fruit unto God."

Do you see that in the scripture above, the oracle of God says to be married to another? You cannot marry yourself. You must marry another, and it says to Christ, the one who rose from the dead. Yet Christ is not marrying one person; He is marrying a group that is called the church of God. Will you be ready? Will you be a part of this great feast? Only God knows, but again, it starts with the church.

The following are more scriptures in support of Christ and His bride (the church or His body).

Revelation 22:17 says, "*17*And the **Spirit and the bride** say, Come. And let him that heareth say, Come. And let him that is athirst come. And whosoever will, let him take the water of life freely."

Matthew 9:15 says, "And Jesus said unto them, **Can the children of the bridechamber mourn**, as long as the bridegroom is with them? But the days will come, when the bridegroom shall be taken from them, and then shall they fast."

John 3:29 says, "He that hath the **bride is the bridegroom**: but the friend of the bridegroom, which standeth and heareth him, rejoiceth greatly because of the bridegroom's voice: this my joy therefore is fulfilled [.]"

John 10:16 says. "And other sheep I have, which are not of this fold: them also I must bring, and they shall hear my voice; and there shall **be one fold (invisible Church), and one shepherd (Christ).**"

John 11:52 says, "And not for that nation only, but that also he should **gather together in one the children of God that were scattered abroad.**"

# 22 - CONCLUSION

As R. C. Sproul said, "Christ is married to the church. He owns the church. The invisible church is espoused to Him."

We need the body. We need the head. Together, we have a perfect union. The motto for the United States of America states, "*E Pluribus Unum*," which is Latin for "one from many." This is also the state of the church.

The body is made up of many members. And from all nations there will be a gathering of His elect, but it starts with your name not only on the roll in heaven but also on a local church body on earth; Thy will be done on earth as it is in heaven.

If any man loves not Christ, that man hates the body. If any man hates the body (church), that man hates Christ.

If this is so, because they are one, then 1 Corinthians 16:22 applies. It says, "If any man love not the Lord Jesus Christ, let him be Anathema Maranatha." A simple translation says if you love not (hate) Christ, you are an Anathema (Cursed).

There will rest a curse and not a blessing on those who hurt the church. As a person is hurt when he touches a cactus so is an individual that comes against the church. No money, prayers, tithing and fasting can change the curse to those who attack the church.

We have gotten away from these facts by becoming more money and power conscious than Christ conscious. But with Christ comes his church. God help us for the attacks that have come over the years, decades and centuries against what Christ loves (body). Let us make up our minds to change our perspective to not only love Christ and our brothers but most importantly His church.

Well, if you love not the church, which is a part of Christ, you must also be an Anathema. Why? Because they are one. You cannot separate the two. They are one. You cannot have the head without having the body.

You cannot love the head and hate the body.

# 23 – STEPS FOR LEAVING or FINDING A CHURCH

- You should not leave without sharing your time, talent, and tithes FAITHFULLY.
- If you were not faithful to the ministry you are leaving, how can you be faithful to the one you are going too?
- Can you ask for a blessing when you leave? As you came before the church to come in, can you come in before the church to leave?
- Misunderstanding or great observation is not a reason for leaving, especially when the leadership sees your point and makes appropriate adjustments.
- Are you better after you left or worse?
- Make an appointment with the pastor to discuss things.
    - Give it a month after the meeting.
    - You should not talk negatively to another person before or after your decision.
- After you leave the church, it should not take more than 6 months to find a new one.
- Don't let personnel issues affect your decision to leave.
- If you can't find a church, **MAYBE** it's time to come back home (Luke 15).
- If you are ripping the former pastor and church, something is wrong.
- Who is going to replace you? If you have no position or responsibility when you leave, then that means you were not plugged in.
- Are you mad about the truth? Guilt should not be the open door for you to move. Do not cause a mutiny.

- If you can't move with love than you can't move.
- Can you come back to the church and sit on the front row without shame or guilt.
- Can you have a homecoming or does your guilt hinder you from visiting the church.

Printed in the United States
132755LV00002B/40-57/P